Instru

M000196012

LET AUGMENTED REALITY CHANGE HOW YOU READ A BOOK

With your smartphone, iPad or tablet you can use the **Hasmark AR** app to invoke the augmented reality experience to literally read outside the book.

1. Download the **Hasmark app** from the **Apple App Store** or **Google Play**

2. Open and select the (vue) option

3. Point your lens at the full image with the (vue) and enjoy the augmented reality experience.

Go ahead and try it right now with the Hasmark Publishing International logo.

ENDORSEMENTS FOR
RESONANT REFLECTIONS

"David Krehbiel is a master musician and wise mentor. In this powerful book, he shares his profound understanding of life, purpose, and ourselves. It will lead you to an extraordinary experience of reality in the continuing present moment of now."

—Don Greene, Ph.D.,
peak performance psychologist and International
Bestselling Author of *Train Your Own Hero*

"David Krehbiel's life journey sparkles with offbeat brilliance. From dyslexic kid to world renown French Horn player, Krehbiel's quest for authenticity and beauty in a world of straight jacketed notions, delights and inspires all of us who have questioned the "sacred idols" of our society. Putting his horn away, David takes time to contemplate the great unknown of our lives and future."

—Paul Buxman,
celebrated artist, musician, activist,
farmer and spiritual teacher

"David Krehbiel has unlocked the secret to life and spirituality! In his second novel *Resonant Reflections*, David presents readers with the tools to understand, accept and better life through meditation, mindfulness and self-realization."

—Judy O'Beirn,
President of Hasmark Publishing International

"Have you ever doubted the veracity of religious dogma and theology handed you from childhood and then been reluctant to voice your uncertainty for fear of rejection from family, friends, and even God? Then take this spiritual odyssey with renowned French horn musician David Krehbiel in his second book, *Resonant Reflections,* as he powerfully and empathetically shares his journey and suggests how it is possible to find assurance of our connection to the Creator, to the Universe, and to each other by learning to exist in the present moment."

—Ruth Anne Krause,
writer and editor

RESONANT REFLECTIONS

A Spiritual Odyssey

DAVID KREHBIEL

With R. A. Krause

Permission should be addressed in writing to David Krehbiel at
adkrehbiel36@gmail.com

Editors: Ruth Anne Krause
         Day Bulger
Cover Design: Anne Karklins anne@hasmarkpublishing.com
Book Design: Amit Dey amit@hasmarkpublishing.com

ISBN 13: 978-1-77482-145-9
ISBN 10: 1774821451

DEDICATION

. . . to anyone who is searching

CONTENTS

POEMS

PRELUDE

Twenty-two years ago, I retired from an extraordinary career—forty years playing principal horn in three major orchestras (the Chicago, Detroit, and San Francisco symphonies) and teaching many wonderful students who are today performing all over the world. Last year I wrote my memoir, *Through the Door: A Horn-Player's Journey,* a story that begins by relating my adventures as a young musician learning to use newly discovered musical talents to cover up scholastic shortcomings. It ends at the finale of my career, a retirement performance of Mozart's Horn Concerto No. 2, my last solo appearance with the San Francisco Symphony Orchestra, and a serenade by forty horn-players outside Davies Symphony Hall before that performance.

I am honored and humbled that *Through the Door: A Horn-Player's Journey* was nominated for several book awards, among them the Eric Hoffer, Indie, and National Book Awards for best memoir. The book was a labor of love in recounting the emotional journey of a career I had thought I could only dream of. I am grateful for the many doors that opened for me during my career. What an adventure it was!

My purpose in writing *Through the Door* was not only to entertain by telling great stories about performing wonderful musical works with famous conductors and artists, but to encourage my readers to go boldly through any door the universe opened to them and accept with gratitude the challenges that await on the other side. After I finished writing the book, I felt there was nothing more to say and that I had finished my short writing career with one book.

When an interviewer asked me if there was anything I wanted to say that wasn't in the book, I was surprised to realize that I actually did have more to say! My life was different now after retiring. During my career, I thought only of performing, conducting, and teaching. I held back sharing the spiritual side of my life—the part where I was born to a Mennonite family, went to church, and had a minister for a grandfather—and much more.

So now I am writing a second book, a meditation on my lifelong quest for answers to spiritual questions such as *Who am I? Why am I here? What is my place in the world? What is actually on the other side of the door I speak of in my first book?* It concerns those years we all have in common, no matter what career we choose, those early years when we are trying to figure things out. The story in this book was written in hopes of encouraging anyone who has been asking tough questions to venture past rigid belief systems on the path to finding something that will lead to greater understanding and peace.

I have always wondered how people can accept a rigid belief system at a certain point and be locked into that system for the rest of their lives; not only that but want to lock others in as well. Everything on the planet is changing and has been forever. To never change beliefs or your concept of how and why we are here on this planet is to stagnate and eventually become obsolete. Witness that there are people who still believe that the earth is flat. To evolve is to change, and I believe that our purpose here is to evolve in our understanding and connection to our Creator, Higher Power, or God. It involves understanding the concept of being ONE WITH EVERYTHING, or that we are all part of God and each other.

Some of the things I have discovered may seem old hat to you. But other things may seem unfamiliar, maybe even at odds with your current thinking and therefore uncomfortable. I hope you won't dismiss them when you come to them. Certainly, we have all taken different paths, but hopefully we can find it within ourselves to remain open to further spiritual insight. Wouldn't it be great to discover the notion of our oneness rather than dwell on our differences? Wouldn't it be wonderful to have a glimpse of that love that can overflow all of us when we are connected? Let's take a "mind walk" together while I share with you my spiritual odyssey.

After rejecting much of the dogma and doctrines of my early religious training, I became influenced by six main sources who I will introduce in this book: Carlos Castaneda, George Gurdjieff, Eckhart Tolle, Steve Taylor, and two channeled entities—Michael and Ra. Again, I'm not asking the reader to believe what I've come to believe, but my journey has given me a workable understanding of who I am and why I'm here in this incarnation on this planet.

I have learned that what lies on the other side of the door, beyond our perceived personal reality, is the opportunity to connect with God or the Higher Power, as some would say. This chance for connection can happen for all of us when we become conscious that it is possible. When we are conscious in the present moment, not letting the voice in our head take us away into the past or future, we can connect to something outside our egoistic personal reality. This, for me, is the essence of meditation. When conscious in the present moment, we can connect with everything on the planet, in the solar system, in the universe, with each other, and ultimately, with God because when existing in the present moment, everything is connected. We are ONE WITH EVERYTHING. Let's explore this miracle of complete presence in the moment. How can we experience it?

I

——— THE OTHER SIDE ——— OF THE DOOR

Spirituality is the connection to a Higher Power.
Religion is a set of beliefs.

As I reflect, I wonder, does feeding religious dogma into a child's formative, uncritical mind close off future independent thinking? The apostle Paul encourages readers (1 Corinthians 13:11) to move beyond childhood thinking and mature into adult thinking. But children are quite literal in their thinking. When told of heaven and who God is, for example, they quite often learn to fear rather than to cultivate a loving relationship with God, with themselves, with others, and with the universe. In addition, they often learn that there are rules to follow without question if they want to go to heaven.

Questioning or thinking critically about the rules and doctrines of Christianity is not often encouraged or nurtured in churches or in any religious training. I have many friends who, even as adults, are hesitant under threat of heaven or hell to venture far from their early Sunday school training when it comes to questioning their beliefs. I have concluded that to connect with God, I need to question my belief systems and forcefully state what is true for me at this time in my life.

When I was a child, the Lord's Prayer, well known to most churchgoing children and adults, enveloped me with its rhythm and its cadence and seemed to make sense. When I thought about the words, with a lot of effort, I could almost make them relevant to my world.

As an adult, I felt my prayers needed to be more relevant. So, in trying to make the Lord's Prayer authentic to me, I created a version that described what was true for me in my present spiritual evolution.

Rewriting the Lord's Prayer takes some chutzpah, by the way! Try it!

Below is my new version of the Lord's Prayer side by side with the conventional one, and I'll explain the changes I made in each verse. My version of the Lord's Prayer may sound strange now, but after reading further in this book, it will possibly sound less so. But my point is, it's okay to question what one has been taught, and it may even help in one's spiritual growth.

THE LORD'S PRAYER

Original   **My Version**

FIRST STANZA

Our Father, who art in   Our Creator, who art
heaven, hallowed be thy   within us, let feeling your
name.   presence be our quest.

I use the word "Creator" (the all-knowing force behind everything—myself, the planet, and the universe) rather than the more formal "Father," which tends to create an image of teacher/student or fatherly authority. The Father is in heaven, but the Creator is within us, and I am asking to always feel that presence.

SECOND STANZA

Thy kingdom come, thy   When we remember we
will be done, on Earth as it   are not in the universe,
is in heaven.   we are the universe, then
                                Earth can be our heaven.

If I am an intrinsic part of the universe and all its dimensions, then God's kingdom is already within me to discover.

THIRD STANZA

Give us this day our daily bread, and forgive us our trespasses as we forgive those who trespass against us.

Give us this day our daily strength, and forgive us our unconsciousness as we forgive those who are ego-bound among us.

It takes a lot of strength to remain in the present during the day. Unconsciousness means being either in the future or the past and out of touch with or separate from the Creator.

FOURTH STANZA

And lead us not into temptation, but deliver us from evil. For thine is the kingdom, and the power, and the glory forever. Amen!

And lead us not into separation, but deliver us from forgetting that within us is God's kingdom, power, and glory, and that we are ONE WITH EVERYTHING!

We become separated from others, God, and ourselves when we forget we are ONE WITH EVERYTHING. *It is important to remember who we are! That's what faith is—remembering.*

Blind faith in church dogma and doctrines without remembering ourselves and our connection to the universe and without examining all the possible reasons for our existence here on the planet is my definition of evil.

We are torn apart by the idea that we should have faith. Faith can be a positive force or a negative force depending on how we use it.

There are 180 degrees of separation between blind faith and the faith of remembering ourselves and our connection to the universe.

What Does It Mean to Be
ONE WITH EVERYTHING?

This morning, while hiking up the hill to my favorite meditation spot beneath an old pine tree, I listened to the crunching of the grains of sand under my feet, observing my footprints being left in that sand.

Stopping under the pine, I looked down at the sand and thought, *I am like one of those tiny grains, each having once been part of a larger rock that had separated itself millions of years ago from a rock that was itself millions of years old.*

As this species on this planet, what insignificant newcomers we are in the cosmic time frame.

We couldn't be more than a few nanoseconds in the life of the universe.

Like the sand, life is a process of development and evolution and quite possibly, like the sand, a separation from our source.

The arrogance of thinking that we are not part of something larger than ourselves separates us from our Creator and our connection to everything.

For me, the way of remembering myself is to realize my time frame on this planet in relation to those grains of sand, and those grains of sand in relation to the universe.

II.

—— THE JOURNEY SO FAR: —— STEPS ALONG THE WAY

Who Am I?

The small, picturesque town of Reedley nestles in the vineyards and orchards along the Kings River in California's central San Joaquin Valley, and the First Mennonite Church on L Street is where my religious training began.

My grandfather, Dr. Henry Krehbiel, a theologian, author, and leading minister of the General Conference of the Mennonite Church, was invited to become the founding pastor of the new church in Reedley. In 1910, he and the rest of the Krehbiel family moved from Ohio to California so he could accept the invitation. This was my grandfather's second pastorate. Beginning in 1892, he had served as pastor of the Mennonite church in Trenton, Ohio.

Much later in life, I became aware of a strange coincidence in that my two grandfathers became acquainted in Kidron, Ohio, long before either of my parents were born. It happened that at the Mennonite Church in Kidron, where Grandfather Gerber was a member, one of the parishioners had committed suicide. The resident pastor of the Kidron church refused to officiate at the service in Kidron since he believed suicide was a sin (as did most practicing Christians).

Grandfather Gerber was part of a group who questioned this belief and began searching for someone who was willing to officiate at the service. They finally found the young Pastor Krehbiel in Trenton. He was willing to travel over two hundred miles to Kidron to officiate at the service. That's where my two grandfathers met, and I have a feeling of warmth when I hear of the inclusiveness of them both, and that the incident was a part of my family so many years ago.

In 1925, Grandfather Krehbiel was the only American delegate to the first Mennonite World Conference in Basel, Switzerland. The conference inspired him to scrape together the resources needed to travel through Europe. Seeing a Europe still devastated by World War I, he became a leader and advocate for nonviolence and world peace and wrote a book, *A Trip Through Europe, A Plea for the Abolition of War, and A Report of the 400th Anniversary of the Denomination*. He was active in founding and promoting a new college in Bluffton, Ohio. In 1930, he received an honorary Doctor of Divinity degree from that college.

I was born in 1936, so I don't remember my grandfather well; he died when I was barely five. But I do remember him as tall and slender, a kind, dignified man with white hair. In his pictures, he reminds me of Mark Twain. I learned from my relatives that he was a charismatic speaker who attracted quite a following of professors and scholars from the local college to his congregation. He gave three services each Sunday: two in English and one in German. The church he pastored grew through the years and remained home for the Krehbiel family.

Maybe it's in the genes, but to this day, I hold two beliefs from my early Christian training. One of these is the commandment, "Thou shall not kill." Our church has zealously followed this commandment for nonviolence through the years. Many of the young men in our congregation became conscientious objectors at draft age. I have always believed that killing for any reason is insane and so is war.

The other commandment that stuck with me was, "Love your neighbor as yourself." This seemed a little harder to follow because of the prevalent feeling of separation we all have toward people different from us. Yet Jesus called the commandment to love one's neighbor as oneself the most important commandment of all.

There were other matters, though, about which I wasn't so certain. These questions remained unanswered, and I would lie in my bed at night pondering, *Who am I? Why am I here? What about my body? Am I a human or am I a machine?* I didn't get acceptable answers to these questions at the time, but I remained certain about one thing: war and killing for any reason were wrong and *not* part of my purpose here. I wondered why humans were so infected with the insanity of war.

Life handed me two roles as a youngster—in church, the grandchild of a preacher, and in school, a scholar. I was always expected to be good at both, yet I didn't feel successful at either. In fact, both church and school were extremely difficult and painful experiences for me.

On Sunday mornings, I sat through Sunday school and church because my parents expected me to. Though I loved the music, the sermons didn't have a lot to do with my life. From my childhood through my teens, Christianity left me with many more questions than answers. In fact, I always felt like even the questions I asked were wrong. We were led to believe that church was a place where all the answers to life's questions could be found with certainty. But church just didn't quite work out that way for me. I developed a feeling that church was a place where certain questions weren't to be asked at all. Schoolteachers and Sunday school teachers alike seemed to think I was being disrespectful when I asked unanswerable questions.

The stories told in Sunday school and church were unbelievable, and no one ever tried to make scientific sense of them, particularly the miracles of raising people from the dead. I was told to just have faith and believe that they were true. It was both frightening and insulting to be told that if I planned to go to heaven, I *must* believe these stories and the dogma implicit in them. I often interrupted the flow with questions, and I really wanted to know the answers to them. *Is God real? Where is he? Are heaven and hell real?* The answers to those questions were always, *Yes, there is a God*, and *Yes, heaven and hell are real because the Bible says so! Read the Bible, and it will give you the answers to all your questions.*

But the question that troubled me most was this: What if someone had never been exposed to Christianity or had never heard the stories or the rules? Was this person going to hell? If so, that seemed very unfair. If there was a loving God, how could he permit this?

I'll never forget the answer to the above question, that it was my responsibility to go into the world and spread the gospel to the unsaved who hadn't yet heard the good news! I knew that was what missionaries did, but telling me that it was my responsibility to spread the gospel presented a big problem.

Even being successful in school was difficult for me. Much later, I found out that I had a handicap, unknown at the time. It was called dyslexia. But, aside from that, I couldn't see myself persuading anyone, especially my friends, that if they didn't believe something that I had trouble believing myself, they were doomed.

To relieve some of my religious frustration, I became quite clever at causing trouble. Often on Sunday evenings, missionaries would present slideshows of their work in foreign lands. The speaker would use a clicker to signal the person operating the slide projector. I showed up with my own clicker and disrupted the whole process for the presenter and tried the patience of the poor missionaries. This was probably a precursor to my later torment of conductors and some of my peers in the world of symphony orchestras as I relate in my first book, *Through the Door*.

As a youth, I felt like a failure, not only as a student but as a Christian, and I never spoke to my parents about how I felt. I just went through the motions. I did get baptized with the other kids in my Sunday school class when we all professed our faith and had our heads doused with a pitcher of water.

In those days, no one knew what dyslexia was, including the teachers. All I knew at the time was that I was haunted by the feeling that I wasn't very smart. For one thing, I felt as though I had something terribly wrong with my memory. Most of the kids at church could remember and recite Bible verses. I couldn't. In school, the other students could spell and recite multiplication tables. But I couldn't remember the multiplication tables, and I couldn't remember how words were spelled. I had to start from scratch with every word, sound out each syllable, and then improvise a spelling. In fact, I felt like I was improvising and faking my way through school.

Even now, I keep a dictionary in my shop so that when I label something, I can spell it correctly. Not being able to spell words correctly, even now, is embarrassing. Fortunately, my wife, Carol, is an excellent speller. Spell check also helps.

The problems I had led me to a core belief that I wasn't going to succeed, and I developed a strong voice in my head that kept reminding me of that! In turn, I felt intimidated by anyone I perceived to be smarter than I, which included just about everyone.

Welcome to the world of dyslexia!

Who knows how many other students in my classes struggled with their memory year after year, feeling "stupid," not knowing there was such a thing as dyslexia?

During an interview about my book *Through the Door,* the interviewer asked me to talk about how dyslexia affected my relationships with my teachers. Relating to teachers was difficult. I thought I wasn't smart, so I avoided talking to them. Also, by not talking to them, I escaped the mortification of not remembering things they'd said in class and then being scolded for not paying attention.

I just always wanted to be left alone to figure things out for myself at my own pace. When I was unable to memorize and recite the times tables like the other students, I figured out a method of my own to calculate them quickly. Years later, when I heard people talking about the new math, I realized I had been using my own primitive version of that.

Later, during my career as a teacher and performer, my favorite students were those who thought of me as a coach and not a do-it-like-I-say teacher. As their coach, I would encourage my students to think, self-analyze, and become their own teachers—solving problems and evolving on their own.

Both church and school became places full of impossible expectations where I couldn't measure up. Since dyslexia was not understood at that time and no one understood my problems, I felt bewildered, left out, and lost much of the time. I think battling dyslexia caused me to be very defensive. I believe my belligerence made it easier to eventually reject the dogma of religion. Fortunately for me, there was one saving grace. . . .

Finding Music

At church, I began to discover a new dimension to my world. Music! I must say, the music at church had a greater influence on me than the doctrines that were offered as answers to my questions.

The Mennonites are known for their singing. Our church had four choirs: the children's choir, the youth choir, the mixed adult choir, and the men's chorus. My father sang in the men's chorus, and I still get shivers when I remember their glorious singing: "The Lord is in His holy temple; let all the earth keep silent." This was followed by a rousing "make a joyful noise unto the Lord all ye lands."

During congregational hymn singing, I felt I was surrounded by a mass choir of four hundred voices singing hymns in four-part harmony. My favorite was the Bach chorale *Jesu, Priceless Treasure*. If there were a heaven, it would surely sound like this! But my favorite of all was the magical sound reverberating from the pipe organ as my mother accompanied the singing.

The church had wonderful acoustics. It does to this day.

Not only did my mother play the pipe organ but she was an accomplished pianist, and our home was filled with music as students streamed in for piano lessons after school until evening. When we went to bed at night, she would play Chopin as we fell asleep.

Music involved my emotions and feelings, and I didn't have to worry about memorizing words or other skills that seemed difficult for me.

At an early age, I had been an unsuccessful piano student, which was a disappointment to my mother. But in the fourth grade, I decided to learn to play the trumpet, and my uncle Victor Gerber, who was a music teacher in Ohio, helped me buy one. I learned it easily because I only had to play one note at a time as opposed to the numerous notes of a chord on the piano, which required all ten fingers. But I had a natural feel for the trumpet. It was something I could excel at, which gave me confidence to try other things.

My parents were supportive, happy for me that music had become part of my life. Before I started high school, they took me to a Fresno State College Orchestra concert and made sure I got a front row seat, which in that auditorium happened to be close to Professor Schwartz, a well-known trumpet teacher. I was thrilled to sit so close and be able to watch his every move. However, my ears caught the sound in front of Schwartz—the sound of Dr. James Winter on the French horn. He was a music professor at Fresno State. I listened in awe, and I knew immediately that the dark, mellow sound of that horn was the sound I wanted to emulate for the rest of my life. I switched from the trumpet to the horn as a freshman in high school and began studying with Dr. Winter. Later I became fascinated with the history of the horn and how it evolved from the hunting horn, which was the prime method of communication during a foxhunt.

The emotional power of my horn short-circuited that pesky voice in my head that told me I wasn't smart and that I wouldn't succeed. I can clearly remember in my preteens playing a 78-rpm recording of Tchaikovsky's Fourth Symphony for the first time (on both sides of many discs). I was so taken with the emotion of the piece that I listened to that symphony over and over until I wore the records out.

The fog in my head began to lift as music worked its magic with me. It became my escape from feelings of inadequacy. But much more, music connected me to something larger than myself, something that I could not name. It felt like a new dimension, something from space where I could soar freely without limits.

My Life as a Performer

The joys I began to experience then and the challenges of performing my favorite orchestral works with the great conductors of the time, such as Fritz Reiner, George Szell, Sir Thomas Beecham, Leopold Stokowski, Erich Leinsdorf, William Steinberg, Seiji Ozawa, Edo de Waart, Herbert Blomstedt, and Michael Tilson Thomas, among many others, became a life I wouldn't trade for any other. An unforgettable experience was my first visit ever to Carnegie Hall at age twenty-two, performing there in my first season with the Chicago Symphony Orchestra. My favorite memory, though, is of a bond that developed with my idol, composer Paul Hindemith, who was guest conductor in my last weeks with the Chicago Symphony shortly before his death. I had fallen in love with his music in high school when we played his Symphonic Metamorphosis at the Interlochen Music Camp.

My tenure with the San Francisco Symphony involved exciting travels and tours to Europe, Russia, Hong Kong, Japan, and Germany with our resident conductors Seiji Ozawa, Edo de Waart, Herbert Blomstedt, and Michael Tilson Thomas. There were many exciting adventures during these times. Once, during the time Maestro Blomstedt served as conductor, we were invited by a good friend of our orchestra, conductor Kurt Masur, to perform a concert in Leipzig, East Germany. We were bused-in for the concert because political tensions were so high in East Germany at the time that we weren't allowed to spend the night in a hotel there. Our host, conductor Kurt Masur, led most of the orchestra on a walk to visit Bach's grave inside St. Thomas Church. Soldiers marched alongside us, seeming to wonder if we were in some kind of demonstration. Our well-known maestro from East Germany assured the authorities that we were his guests and harmless. As we entered the church, Bach organ music surrounded us. Maestro Masur had arranged to have the church organist play for us as we arrived. Many of us were in tears as we stood around Bach's resting place surrounded by Bach's music.

Along with my symphony career, I was able to perform and conduct brass ensembles, such as the Summit Brass and Bay Brass, and for a short time, I was a member of the L.A. Brass Quintet. I also conducted large brass ensembles wherever I taught, including Wayne State University, the San Francisco Conservatory of Music, the Music Academy of the West in Santa Barbara, and the Colburn School in Los Angeles.

However, the pressure I faced in performing at that level was so constant that once, while driving to Orchestra Hall in Chicago, I wished to be in a traffic accident rather than face performing that night. I knew that survival in my career meant learning to control my anxiety.

Later in this book, I recount some of the ideas and meditations that helped me overcome or control the anxieties inherent in my career and my life. It is a gift to be able to share them.

After surviving this career, I realized that when given the choice, I much preferred being scared to death than bored to death. Welcome to the world of stage fright!

Connecting to the Universe

(The Lord's Prayer Stanza 1)
Our Creator, who art within us,
let feeling your presence be our quest.

As music became my world, hearing certain music was a spiritual experience, a connection with something much larger than myself, like listening to the old 78-rpm Tchaikovsky recordings. I can remember the same otherworldly experience the first time I heard the Berlioz *Symphonie Fantastique*. Most of us have experienced these moments—maybe in nature or with the birth of a child—where something was so beautiful, so perfect, that we felt at ONE WITH EVERYTHING. If you are a meditator, you recognize this also as the essence of meditation, or of being completely in the present.

Music has given me many of these extraordinary experiences over my lifetime. I am transported to a different plane of existence when incredible music is performed in a way that opens up new vistas of musical emotion—such as when I listen to my favorite recording of Beethoven's

Moonlight Sonata. At these times, the connection between the listener, the performer, and the composer becomes an esoteric experience of oneness. The slightest unexpected nuance in the performance can take one's breath away. The otherworldliness of music was my opening to the possibility of an alternative dimension we can experience while living in our own personal reality. Music is more than just notes. It has an emotional power that is magic. I know I am struggling to put this otherworldliness into words, but this is how music was used in the early church before it became a form of entertainment. You'd enter a cathedral and be moved by the incredible architecture, which together with the music would take you to a dimension that was outside your personal reality. I like to call this feeling connecting to God and the universe. Some music today can still do that.

If we can look at our existence here on the planet as an intrinsic part of the whole universe rather than being separate and unique, we can create access to that other dimension. When we step through that door and pry ourselves away from our small personal reality, we open ourselves to the universe and oneness with it. The feeling of separation disappears. Some call this enlightenment.

Leaving Religion

As I gained access to the new dimensions offered by music, the dogmas of religion began to fade and make even less sense than they had in Sunday school. The idea of the world having been created in seven days, which completely negates archeology as a science, was unacceptable for me. In college, I was able to free myself from this indoctrination enough to question without intimidation the belief systems that were handed me as a youth, often referred to as "The Truth."

Fundamentalist beliefs cause separation. You must believe in the virgin birth, that the Bible is the only true word of God, and that Jesus died to save us from our sins. A true believer does not question fundamental beliefs.

The religion of my youth saw the worship of Jesus, Son of God, as the way to heaven and life after death. Good works, helping the poor and downtrodden, and loving your neighbor were important, but being a true believer, no questions asked, and having faith that you were right were of prime importance. These mindsets have caused enmity and war, as seen through the ages.

Belief and faith were the keys to heaven and eternal life. They seemed more important than evolving to change our level of consciousness here on Earth. Eternal life was waiting for us up there in heaven if we believed the right dogma. Those who didn't would be left behind, as in the books by Tim LaHaye and Jerry B. Jenkins. Jesus reacted to the unconsciousness of religion by throwing the money changers out of the temple. If you read further in this book, you will see that my present understanding of Christianity is completely different from the Christianity I understood as a youth.

However, there is one radical doctrine from my Mennonite youth that has remained with me to this day: non-violence. The Anabaptist belief in pacifism and the belief that all killing is wrong was strongly held in the Mennonite faith and still is. This is different from the fundamentalist dogma I've been talking about. We were looked down on for these beliefs by other Christian denominations where patriotism took precedence. This also occurs when loyalty to your political affiliation takes precedence over what is spelled out in our constitution and the Bill of Rights.

Much later in my life, I began to realize that the Jesus I thought I knew in my youth was not the Jesus I was beginning to discover through the study of different philosophies and religions. The picture of a Caucasian-looking, mild-mannered, loving shepherd holding his staff, surrounded by his sheep, who was mainly concerned with helping us get to heaven has been replaced for me by a Jewish-looking political radical and revolutionary concerned with helping us understand our relationship to God here in the present on the planet.

It began to dawn on me that the pure teachings of Jesus, Buddha, and the founders of other major religions had been politicized, added to, interpreted, and distorted to intimidate and control as in *thou shalt* and *thou shalt not*, and so on.

I enjoyed the movie *Amadeus*. The emperor in the movie, when asked about his objection to Mozart's music, said, "Too many notes!"

For me, the religion of my youth was, "Too many words!" Not to mention, "Too many things to believe."

I think that is what happens with religion. We strive so hard to understand and to make it relevant to our lives that we get caught up with the details and lose sight of the big picture, or the simplification of the concept.

Kelly Johnson, lead engineer at Lockheed, coined the phrase, "Keep it simple, stupid!" From scientific concepts to religious beliefs, the simpler the product or explanation, the more likely it will be useful. The question is, does it make the world a better place? Does it raise our consciousness about how we live in this universe?

When I left for college, I not only left the church I grew up in, but with it, the Christianity and religious beliefs of my childhood and all religion in general. In doing so, I gave up caring about whether I'd go to heaven. I felt that religion had done more harm than good, not only for me but for our planet. I had still never mentioned my feelings about church and Christianity to my family or anyone else. I was sensitive to their sincere feelings and beliefs, and I didn't want to hurt them by my rejection of those beliefs.

It seemed to me that religious beliefs and dogmas throughout history had brought about conflict and war between one religion and another and between one faction of a religion and another. Just look at the sufferings of the souls on the planet. If there was a loving God, would he be letting that happen? In fact, at this point in my life, I was quite angry with formalized and organized religion in general because of the separation and suffering it had caused on the planet. Religious persecution has been an ongoing tragedy through the ages.

III.

———— ON CREATIVE ————
NOT CARING

The great shaman, J. Krishnamurti, when asked his secret, told his followers that it was simply, "I don't mind what happens." I have learned that this means surrendering to the present and not floating away to the past or future.

After walking away from church, religion, and all my incessant youthful questioning, every ounce of my life's energy was taken up with music and trying to learn how, with all my insecurities, I could become comfortable in the world of performing and expressing music. I no longer had time or energy to give to esoteric questioning unless it involved music. Music had presented a new dimension for me, and I didn't feel I needed anything else.

I had a wonderful three years at Fresno State despite flunking "bonehead" English. I studied horn with Dr. James Winter and joined the newly formed Fresno Philharmonic as a freshman.

Dr. Winter was the reason I switched from the trumpet to the horn as a freshman in high school. I never turned back.

In my junior year in college, I had the opportunity to perform the Britten *Serenade for Tenor, Horn and Strings* at College of the Pacific in Stockton, California. I have since played the *Serenade* many times, and it is a favorite. I performed on the first half of the program as scheduled, but then, because the soloist for the second half was sick, the conductor asked me to repeat the Britten after the intermission since it was such a favorite with the audience. I was challenged. It was an opportunity to see if I could do something that difficult twice on the same program. The text for the tenor is based on poems depicting every emotion, with powerful interactions between the tenor and the horn. Whenever I performed the piece, I was so in tune with those emotions that I would forget it was difficult. After all, playing the horn is learning to live on the edge.

In my senior year, at the urging of my teacher, I transferred to Northwestern University in Evanston, Illinois, to study horn with Philip Farkas, the legendary teacher and principal horn of the Chicago Symphony. Also an author, Farkas wrote *The Art of French Horn Playing,* which is known to horn students as "the Bible."

I was astounded when I heard the Chicago Symphony for the first time. I had never heard such playing! "I will never be able to play like that!" said the voice in my head.

I did know I'd have to work hard if I wanted a career at that level. It became my quest to discover how to play consistently with that ability and to gain freedom from performance anxiety. We, as performers, are asked to pull ourselves up by the bootstraps. At the highest level, we walk a tightrope without a safety net. We take a huge leap of faith. This level of orchestral playing happens in most major orchestras as a given. It's what people pay to experience and what we, as players, take for granted most of the time.

Shortly after beginning my studies with Farkas, he surprised me by arranging an audition with the maestro of the Chicago Symphony Orchestra, Dr. Fritz Reiner. The audition was to be held at Reiner's apartment. I'd heard the horror stories about Reiner and knew that if I missed one note or showed any weakness, I would fail the audition.

I arrived at the apartment tower, took the elevator up to his floor, and knocked at his door, petrified. The short, stocky maestro opened the door himself, blinked up at me over half-moon glasses, and motioned me in.

"What would you like me to play?" I asked as I sat down and took out my horn.

"Play *Heldenleben*!" he growled at me. (*Ein Heldenleben* is a tone poem by Richard Strauss that begins with solo horn and cellos on a low written B-flat.)

It was cold out, mid-December, and I hadn't played a note yet that day. When I tried to play the low B-flat, there was no sound, only air. I laid my horn in my lap, sat, and waited for him to tell me to leave. But instead, he walked over to the credenza next to me and began thumbing slowly through a book. I could see it was my teacher Farkas's new book on the art of French horn playing. He found the place and held it with his thumb as he said to me, "Your teacher says you must loosen the embouchure for the low notes," which, for me, was a major FGOTO (Firm Grasp Of The Obvious). Then he told me to try it again. This time, the note sounded, and I was able to relax. I figured I had already failed the audition. But something was different. I continued to play the rest of the audition excerpts but without my normal anxiety. Then I left, convinced I had failed because of that first note.

A week later, I got a phone call. When I answered, someone said, "Congratulations! You are a new member of the Chicago Symphony Orchestra. You will be starting next September, but we need you to come in now and play with us for a few weeks as an extra."

Wow! Here I was, a college student who was suddenly catapulted into the major league of orchestras!

Maybe even more important than being hired by the CSO was what I had learned from that auditioning experience with Reiner. In that audition, I had inadvertently discovered the perfect attitude for auditioning, performing, and maybe even living. After not being able to play the first note, I assumed that I had failed the audition. So I let myself relax and enjoyed playing the rest of the audition without caring about the outcome. In that state, I was able to play freely, fully experiencing the emotion of the music. This perfect auditioning attitude had happened by accident, but I realized that maybe I could learn to call it up at will. I retired to the practice rooms at Northwestern University, where I began developing ways into this attitude, which I decided to call Creative Not Caring.

Creative Not Caring simply means, *I am not affected by what I just did, and I am not thinking about what I am about to do. I reside only in the present. Then, in the present, I focus intently on feeling and communicating the emotion of the music.*

Continually being present in the moment while performing frees one from the voice that creeps into the head and creates anxiety. Most of us are probably aware of a voice like that. The idea of Creative Not Caring became my way of staying in the present as a solo performer and ignoring that pesky voice. The purpose of that voice, I suppose, was to protect my ego from damage, but the truth was that it pulled me away from the present and from being completely involved with what I was doing at that moment.

I noticed that I was always thinking, and what I thought controlled my emotions. Learning to identify the voice in my head that created performance anxiety was a gift. I used to think that voice was telling the truth when it told me I wasn't smart enough or good enough. But in Creative Not Caring, I learned to control how I responded to that voice, if not entirely control the content of what it told me.

If I used my mind to stay involved with the feeling of the music at every moment, I could control the voice that wondered how I was doing or if I would be able to do what came next. Creative Not Caring neutralizes that voice. Creative Not Caring became my way of staying present while remaining connected to the emotion of the music. Denying that ego-voice made auditioning and performing a challenge that I looked forward to and not something I dreaded. Performance began to be a process of self-discovery.

As always, striving to understand and be my own teacher, I've found a few tips that have helped me over the years to stay in the present while performing. You also might find them useful.

Becoming Present When Performing

- When performing, try feeling the magnetism between one note and the next. Realize that notes aren't isolated from each other, but that one note is pregnant with feeling that gives birth to the next note. Or one phrase is pregnant with feeling that gives birth to the next phrase. There is a feeling of tension and release, suspension and relaxation, as in inhaling and exhaling. This is what gives music life. When listening to music, you can feel that quality.

- There is much pleasure in having to wait for the completion of something you have already heard in your mind. The essence of musicality is catching the ears of the listeners in a way that connects them as if they were composing the music and performing with you.

- Every note has a purpose. It's either going someplace or returning someplace. There are no nude notes or notes that don't have a purpose going or coming, intensifying or relaxing, or having an emotional value relating to everything around them.

- A great performance captures the consciousness of the listener. It keeps the voice in the head of the listener from leaving the present moment. I always say that while performing, we must grab the listener firmly by the ears and not let go.

Hearing the Voice inside Your Head

At the time I developed Creative Not Caring in my senior year at Northwestern, my interest was only in controlling performance anxiety by focusing on the emotion of the music while staying in the present moment. During my years in San Francisco, I began studying different spiritual disciplines. I soon realized that the method I called Creative Not Caring, with its focus on remaining in the present, was similar in concept to ancient schools of meditation and, more recently, to other teachings, such as those of Eckhart Tolle in *The Power of Now* and *A New Earth*.

Tolle teaches that we all have a voice in our heads that is controlled by our egos. With dyslexia, I'd heard it loudly all my life! Sometimes, the voice battered me with self-doubt and worry, telling me that what I was doing wasn't good enough and that I would fail. Most of the time, the voice chattered judgmentally, taking me from the present into obsessing about the future or the past. Residing in the present keeps the voice at bay.

At an early age, I tried to discover who and what this voice was by deconstructing it. Were there two parts of me—the voice and the machine? Or were there three parts of me—the machine (my body), the voice, and the part of me that is aware of that voice (or an observer)? Could I separate myself from it? Could it control me?

Decades later, I discovered that Eckhart Tolle calls this voice the "ego voice" and says that residing in the present moment gives one freedom from that voice of the ego.

Being constantly aware of the voice in our daily lives as well as in performing music is a real challenge. Later in my career, I began the practice of meditation when I joined the Gurdjieff group in San Francisco. Meditation always makes me painfully aware of how that voice takes me away from the present into the past or the future. Staying in the present takes practice.

If you would like to learn to quiet that voice and exist in the present moment, I suggest practicing the following sitting meditation. Practicing meditation strengthens concentration and focus by neutralizing the voice in your head.

Presence: A Meditation

1. Sitting in a comfortable position, make sure the body is relaxed. Close your eyes. Breathe deeply. Observe the breath and pay attention to how it feels as it flows in and out. Keep feeling and paying attention with each breath.

2. Whenever your attention goes elsewhere, just notice it and escort the attention back to the breath. When that voice takes you to the past or the future, when that voice in your head creates fear and anxiety, when that voice in your head creates negative emotion, come back to the present, come back to the now. If your mind leaves 100 times, then calmly bring it back 101 times.

3. By doing this, you are training your mind to be less reactive. You are in the present, taking each moment

as it comes, not valuing any one moment above the other. By repeatedly bringing your attention back to the breath each time it wanders, you are building and deepening your mind's ability to concentrate. You are becoming nonjudgmental. You are practicing residing in the present. In these quiet moments, you connect with the Creator, the universe, or your higher self, whichever of these is meaningful for you. You are disconnecting from the ego voice, the voice that always brings separation from something bigger than yourself.

Remain in this state for as long as you feel comfortable doing so, even if it's only three to five minutes. When you can, increase the time until you can sit in the present focusing on your breathing for twenty to thirty minutes.

It's ironic, isn't it, that practicing Creative Not Caring while meditating can *reverse* that voice in the head and help you get back to the present moment. Focusing on these poems while meditating can aid in that reversal of the voice.

The Reversal

When the voice in your head takes you to the past or the future
When the voice in your head creates fear and anxiety

When the voice in your head creates negative
emotion
    Come back to the present
    Come back to the now
    Come back to what you really are.

—by David Krehbiel

Presence

Being in the present is a gift.
My joy of living now is in this quest.
A demanding spiritual journey it is,
watching one's thoughts go by.
Being aware of my thoughts, not
letting myself drift into the future or the past,
brings me closer to understanding my
relationship to a Higher Power.

—by David Krehbiel

The Voice inside Your Head

One day you'll grow fed up with the voice inside
your head
with its constant murmurings of discontent
its fearmongering thoughts of the future
and its questioning of every choice you make.

One day you'll turn to it and calmly say, "I refuse
to listen"
then stand back and look away
turning your attention to your surroundings
or to a quietness and spaciousness you can sense
inside you, just behind the voice.

The voice is so self-absorbed
that at first it won't even notice it's being ignored
and will carry on chattering away to itself.
You'll still hear its complaints and criticisms
but they won't convince you anymore—
you'll doubt them, laugh at them, reject them.

And gradually, without the fuel of your attention,
the voice will become more hesitant
will stumble and slow down, leaving space;

until eventually that self-assertive drawl
that demanded to be heard
and seemed to submerge the rest of reality
will be no louder than a whisper, like a gentle breeze
that seems to be part of silence.

—by Steve Taylor[1]

If you're having trouble staying present during meditation, it might be helpful to use a guided meditation.

I've turned my version of the Lord's Prayer into a guided meditation that helps me focus and be present in my body. Below is my current regimen. Remember, my meditation regimen is a suggestion only as there are many ways to still your mind and connect with the power of the universe. Finding your own path to a Higher Power can be rewarding for you and the consciousness of the planet.

By the way, when you do find your mind wandering during meditation, think of it as positive rather than negative because becoming conscious of a wandering mind is a sign of being conscious or aware at a new level.

The Lord's Prayer Revisited

Our Creator, who art within us,
let feeling your presence be our quest.

When we remember we are not in the universe,
we are the universe,
then Earth can be our heaven.

Give us this day our daily strength, and
forgive us our unconsciousness
as we forgive those who are ego-bound among us.

And lead us not into separation, but
deliver us from forgetting that

within us is God's kingdom, power, and glory,
and that we are ONE WITH EVERYTHING!

The Meditation

First, after relaxing and scanning for tension in any part of
my body, I say these two short prayers.

Prayer 1. (The poet uses the word *sun* as a metaphor for
God, universe, and Higher Power.)

> I AM One, I AM One, I AM One with the Sun.
> I AM One, I AM One with the Great Central Sun.
>
> God is here in my heart. I AM One with God's heart.
> Light, expand through my heart. Love, expand
> through my heart.
> Let my aura be thine. Let my aura now shine.
> O, my God, I AM thine! I AM truly divine!
> We are One, we are One, we are One, we are One.
> We are One, we are One in the Great Central Sun.

—Anonymous[2]

Prayer 2.
> Beloved, I AM love divine,
> Blaze your light, around me shine.
> Cosmic secret rays of fire
> Pulsing, flowing, you inspire.

Violet joy now smile through me,
Raise me up and set me free.
Singing, spinning, burning bright,
Grace me in your mercy light.

—by The Hearts Center[3]

Meditation. While saying each of the four stanzas in the above version of the Lord's Prayer, place your consciousness on each of the four corners of the body, as explained below.

Stanza 1.

Our Creator, who art within us,
let feeling your presence be our quest.

1. Starting with the right arm, place your consciousness on the head and lungs, take a deep breath through the nose, and exhale with pursed lips through the mouth. Silently recite the first stanza.

2. Move to the right leg with consciousness on internal organs. Take a breath and repeat Stanza 1.

3. Move to the left leg with consciousness on the digestive tract. Breathe. Repeat Stanza 1.

4. Move to the left arm with consciousness on the heart and blood circulation. Breathe. Repeat Stanza 1.

Stanza 2.

> *When we remember we are not in the universe,*
>   *we are the universe,*
>   *then Earth can be our heaven.*

Following the sequence for Stanza 1, repeat Stanza 2 with consciousness on right leg, then left leg, left arm, right arm.

Stanza 3.

> *Give us this day our daily strength, and*
>   *forgive us our unconsciousness*
>   *as we forgive those who are ego-bound among us.*

Repeat Stanza 3 with consciousness on left leg, then left arm, right arm, right leg.

Stanza 4.

> *And lead us not into separation, but*
>   *deliver us from forgetting that*
>   *within us is God's kingdom, power, and glory,*
>   *and that we are* ONE WITH EVERYTHING!

Repeat Stanza 4 with consciousness on left arm, then right arm, right leg, left leg.

Repeat the above sequences two more times each, which should take about one half-hour.

You Are Not the Process

Sometimes it's demeaning to watch thoughts pass by
and realize how judgmental and petty they can be.
It's like being sober at a drunken party
cringing as friends make fools of themselves.

"Can this really be me?" you ask yourself, ashamed.
"Is my mind really so full of nonsense?"

But whoever said these thoughts were yours?
Thinking is a process that takes place inside you
like digestion or the circulation of your blood.
And you are not your thoughts
any more than you are your digestion.

Pay as little attention to your thoughts
as you do to your circulating blood.
Take the content of your thoughts as seriously
as the contents of your intestines.

And soon your thoughts will slow down and fade away
into a background noise that doesn't disturb you
like the hum of a small television set, turned down low
flickering in a corner of a room.

And then you'll look inside yourself
and find nothing to be ashamed of.

—by Steve Taylor[4]

IV

—— STEPPING UP THE ——
SEARCH: WHO AM I NOW?

I wonder who I am now that I've given up any pretense of religion yet am learning to connect to a Higher Power.

Am I an Atheist?

An atheist denies the existence of a supreme being or beings. But I have nothing against the presence of a supreme being and, through meditation, am beginning to understand my connection to a Higher Power.

Am I an Agnostic?

An agnostic holds that it is impossible to know if there is an ultimate cause or a God and that human knowledge is limited to what we can experience with our five senses. Maybe we are all wandering the planet on our own with no plan at all!

When I meditate on the night sky gazing up at the stars, my answer to the agnostic is that there must be a plan.

There must be something more to this existence than what we have come to understand with our five senses alone.

College professor and psychic researcher Don Elkins in *The Law of One: Book I: The Ra Material* tells us that when gazing at the stars in the sky at night, we can know that each of those stars is a sun like our own.[1]

The enormity of our universe is unimaginable. In our galaxy alone, there are sixty suns for each living person on Earth today. Light traveling twenty-three earth diameters per second takes four years to reach us from our nearest star and one hundred thousand years to reach us from the most distant star in our galaxy.

"That is a big backyard!" says Elkin.

It would seem ample for even the most ambitious of celestial architects, but in truth this entire galaxy of over two hundred billion stars is just one grain of sand on a very big beach. There are uncounted trillions of galaxies like ours, each with its own billions of stars, spread throughout what seems to be infinite space. When you think of the mind-boggling expanse of our creation and the infantile state of our knowledge in relation to it, you begin to see the necessity for considering the strong probability that our present scientific approach to investigating these expanses is as primitive as the dugout canoe.[2]

One might say that the creation of a distinct system as large as our universe would need a plan by an infinite Creator or force that, in our stage of evolution, we are far from being able to comprehend.

Should I Be a Unitarian Universalist?

I think I knew from an early age that I wasn't an atheist, a person who believes there is no God. It had always seemed obvious to me that there was some plan to our existence, some force in charge.

As I became more comfortable in my profession, I began to look again for answers to my questions. *Who am I? Why am I here?* In the Detroit Symphony Orchestra at that time, I felt like a worker in a musical assembly line. Our performances in the DSO felt ordinary and uninspired. Many of us from the orchestra had done back-up sessions at Motown, which were always fun and inspiring. So eight of us from the orchestra created a fusion rock group, Symphonic Metamorphosis, combining classical music with popular rock. We composed our own music, which enabled us to be more creative. We performed many concerts and were often featured soloists with the DSO. We also made two recordings with London Records. In a way, we broke the barrier between classical music and rock and roll.

During this time, I began to reach out beyond my horn-playing cocoon, becoming more conscious of what was going on outside the world of music. I was concerned with human rights and race relations, particularly the Detroit riots and the grape boycotts. The grape boycotts involved my wife's family in California. My father-in-law, Roy Smeds, became the first grape grower in the Reedley area to sign a contract with the United Farm Workers Union. He drove to Delano and completely surprised Cesar Chavez and Dolores Huerta. As a union contractor, he paid his workers more, and his grapes became union grapes, but he was ostracized for his radical stance on farm labor by most of the farmers in the area, who were very conservative.

While becoming more other-oriented, I still searched for answers to my questions, *Who am I?* and *Why am I here?* I started attending a Unitarian Universalist church. It seemed a safe place for people like me who wanted to be connected to serving the planet without having to be attached to religious dogma. The Unitarians seemed genuine in their concern for our plight as a species on this planet. Race, religion, and sexual orientation made no difference in their belief that we were all one.

With the Unitarians, I became aware of the idea of oneness or unity. Since we were all connected, it was our responsibility to work at making our planet a better place to live. I was finally realizing there were many souls before me who understood this idea of oneness and that it was our egos that separated us from each other and from a Higher Power. Some of these souls offered esoteric teachings that had been hidden in plain sight for centuries, and I made it my quest to get to know them.

V.

———— CONNECTING ————
WITH THE UNIVERSE:
GUIDES ALONG THE WAY

New Dimensions

There is a great divide between our personal reality, or our ego, and experiencing a connection with the universe. When we step through the door of our personal reality into oneness with the universe, we experience a new dimension full of possibilities. Our lives open to a personal connection with a Higher Power and maybe even a "peace that surpasses all understanding."

As I began my search for new dimensions with the books of Carlos Castaneda, I became excited about the thought that there might be a reality we could experience beyond our five senses.

(The Lord's Prayer Stanza 2)
When we remember we are not in the universe,
we are the universe,
then Earth can be our heaven.

Carlos Castaneda

Castaneda teaches that, "One cannot judge nonordinary realities with either-or lenses." Castaneda's lessons taught that there is much in this gigantic universe that is beyond our current understanding.

Castaneda (1925–1998) wrote a series of books that describe his spiritual odyssey while being trained in shamanism under the tutelage of Don Juan Matus, whom Castaneda called a Yaqui man of knowledge. With Matus as his teacher, Castaneda became a nagual, or a sorcerer/shaman who was able to shift into animal form through magic rituals or psychoactive drugs. Nagual refers to that part of perception that is in the realm of the unknown yet still reachable by humankind. Castaneda referred to this realm as nonordinary reality. His books tell of his odyssey into this reality of dealing with more than one dimension.

Since I had rejected religion, music had become my way of connecting spiritually with God and other people. I was ready now for a new dimension. The idea that there was something in our universe that was beyond the five senses—seeing, hearing, smelling, tasting, and touching—was an intriguing concept, and Castaneda was a stepping-stone into this new dimension.

Even the Bible mentions other dimensions and realities when speaking of heaven. Heaven was always a mystery to me and a place I would go if I obeyed the rules. Is heaven real? The answer was always, *Yes, because the Bible says so.*

In fact, according to the Bible, there are many heavens. Deuteronomy 10:14 explains that ". . . the highest heavens belong to the Lord your God, also the earth with all that is in it."[1]

Also, the Bible refers to the many levels of heaven in 1 Kings 8:27: "But will God indeed dwell on the earth? Behold, heaven and the heaven of heavens cannot contain [God]."[2]

In John 1:51, Jesus promises his disciple Nathaniel, "You shall see heaven open, and the angels of God ascending and descending upon the Son of Man."[3]

Observing without Judgment

I noticed at one point that I had become a very black-and-white, either-or, true-or-false thinker. There were good people and bad people, good players and not-so-good players, good-looking people and not-so-good-looking people. I seemed to have a judgment about everything.

I started to wonder, Was this judgment yet another form of belief system that was being run by my ego?

Good question! But I'd certainly become judgmental! My ego was quite happy with this arrangement, though. I used to have all the questions; now I had all the answers. I had become right and everyone else wrong. This state of mind brought about an ego-driven separation from everything.

My judgmental attitude grew, permitting me to bolster my fragile ego. Feeling superior, I suppose, eased my battle with dyslexia and helped protect me from the constant pressure of competition inherent in my profession. I clearly recalled the first time I realized that the best players were not always the best people, and the best people were not always the best players. That was the beginning of the end of my black-and-white world!

> *The moment that judgment stops through acceptance of what is, you are free of the mind. You have made room for love, for joy, for peace.*
>
> —Eckhart Tolle[4]

Castaneda's writings negated my judgmental black-and-white, either-or approach to reality.

One can't enter non-ordinary realities while judging them through either-or-lenses. I began finding that there were many levels of reality and many ways of viewing them. Can two people have contrasting opinions about a viewed reality and both be right? Or can two mutually exclusive things exist at the same time in the same place? We've probably all experienced unexplainable phenomena, at least on simple levels, and thought of them as coincidences or synchronicities.

A friend of mine has a beautiful home in the hills of Oakland, California. He lamented that his neighbor's large tree blocked a view of the bay. Late last summer, an afternoon thunderstorm blew through the area with heavy rain and wind gusts. As he sat in his living room listening to the rain pound his windows, he was startled by a loud crack. This was followed by a deafening thud as the neighbor's huge tree crashed onto his roof. Was this a catastrophe? Or was it a miracle? It depends on how you see it. The Zen master would react to these events by being totally neutral: "Is that so?"

After the tree was removed from the top of his house and the roof repaired, he realized he now had a coveted view of the San Francisco Bay. Plus, he no longer had to deal with all those messy leaves on his roof and in his yard.

It's possible that what we experience or observe at a certain place and time may not be the only possible reality. Might this also be true of religious dogma we've learned?

A Different Way of Seeing

In Carlos Castaneda's story of his teacher's journey to Ixtlan, Don Juan tells him, "So when you're trying to figure it out, all you're really doing is trying to make the world familiar. You and I are right here, in the world that you call real, simply because we both know it."[5] Might this concept be true of Christian, Jewish, Catholic, or any other beliefs we hold onto in order to be secure or right?

Don Elkins (quoted in Chapter 4) writes that Einstein's declaration about everything being relative is so apt, it has become a cliché. "Let us continue being relativistic," says Elkins, "in considering the size of natural phenomena by considering the size of our galaxy." In the huge expanse of our universe, it's probable that there are realities other than what we already know and that these realities behave in ways we've not seen before. Considering this, is it possible that we can observe our current realities without a true or false judgment?

Though the Bible has many truths, there are realities that extend beyond the Bible. There are many ancient and modern esoteric writings, for example, that are available to us now because of our twenty-first century access to information and history, yet they are still hidden from most of us. It is possible the writings of some of the individuals and groups in the next few chapters could be among these.

George Ivanovich Gurdjieff

Gurdjieff (1866–1949) was an Armenian guru, mystic, writer, and composer. Both Castaneda and Gurdjieff focused on waking people up to the possibility of alternate realities. They were my stepping-stones into that new reality on the other side of the door.

During the COVID-19 pandemic, we were asked to extend the time we washed our hands to the time it took to sing

> Row, row, row your boat
> gently down the stream.
> Merrily, merrily, merrily, merrily,
> life is but a dream.

"Merrily, merrily, merrily, merrily" is really a wonderful philosophy in itself! Wouldn't we all like to spend our days merrily rowing down the stream with the breeze at our backs? One day the song popped into my mind and formed an earworm. Every time I would get to the line "life is but a dream," I would think of Gurdjieff because this line summarizes Gurdjieff's philosophy that mankind naturally exists in a dreamlike state.

The Gurdjieff philosophy concentrates on knowing ourselves and the possibility of waking up from our dreamlike state into being how the universe designed us to be. The universe is asking us to evolve.

Gurdjieff asks us to become conscious of that automatic ego-driven voice in our heads that tells us what reality is and keeps us from connecting to anything bigger than ourselves. Gurdjieff taught that people live their entire lives in a state of hypnotic sleep generated by that incessant voice. He developed a method designed to work one's way out of this hypnosis into a higher state of consciousness, eventually activating one's full human potential. This activity was called "the Gurdjieff Work."

I joined a Gurdjieff group while I was playing in the San Francisco Symphony. Membership in the group involved attending meetings, meditating (called "sittings"), and sacred dancing (called "movements"). There were also workdays where we spent the day being with others, trying to do what was called "remembering yourself." For me, this meant being aware of the automatic thinking, or the voice in my head that took me away from the present. Do these ideas begin to sound familiar?

When I was still a beginner in this Work, I received permission to attend a special meeting with Lord Pentland, head of the Gurdjieff Work in the US. I was told not to say anything since I was new to the Work. When it came time for questions, I couldn't help myself. I asked, "How does love fit into this Work?" Well, there was dead silence in which I seemed to have offended everyone in the room. The absence of the idea of love in this room gave me great food for thought.

The Work seemed to be a very serious proposition. However, as usual, I felt that I was left with more questions than answers. The answers to my driving questions, *Who are we?* and *Why are we here?* were vague. But self-help, self-knowledge, and being responsible for ourselves and how we are relating to the universe seemed to be the emphasis rather than love. Would it be possible to connect to a Higher Power through love only? I wonder.

I began meditating regularly when I joined the Gurdjieff group. Constant awareness of that voice in our daily lives is the real challenge. The practice of meditation always makes me painfully aware of that voice and how it takes me away from the present moment into moments past or future. Staying in the present takes practice. Meditation is a most important practice for recognizing that voice in your head and what it can do.

Meeting Michael: Channeling from Another Dimension

As far as answers are concerned, I went from famine to feast. In the next step, I became involved with a small group that was channeling a benevolent conglomerate entity that called itself Michael. Michael was willing to communicate and answer questions brought by the group. Michael was almost too much of a good thing because we could ask anything, and I mean *anything*, and get logical, believable, and fascinating answers to questions about such things as past lives, medical issues, and overleaves (explained below) of anyone we knew, living or dead.

Our early prime questions had to do with who we were, not only in this life but in past lives. Each member of the group could get answers to just about any question they were brave enough to ask. These insightful answers were a veritable feast of knowledge. Several books have been written about this group and the knowledge that was given. The best overall view would be in *Messages from Michael: 25th Anniversary Edition* by Chelsea Quinn Yarbro.

Could it possibly be that we have had many past lives on a long journey with many of the same souls, and that even now we are in contact with souls who, in past lives, have been our brothers and sisters, mothers and fathers, and close friends? We have things to learn from these people, some with whom we have karmic connections carried into our present lives. Each life is a growing and learning experience.

Michael helps people look at their lives with a broad view that brings love and understanding toward all souls. He gives detailed explanations of the basic questions about who we are and why we are here. He opens the door to the possibility that maybe this life is only one small portion of our soul's existence through many lifetimes and proposes that each soul starts its journey through its lifetimes with one of what he calls seven roles in essence.

ESSENCE ROLES

Sage-Artisan
Priest-Slave
King-Warrior
Scholar

These essence roles remain the same through each lifetime. However, the soul does age over many incarnations, progressing from infant through baby, young, mature, and finally, old soul, at the end of which we move to another dimension. At each incarnation, the soul chooses a set of overleaves, which are devices that allow the soul to experience all that is necessary to accomplish a full evolution through the many lifetimes on the physical plane.[6]

Being conscious of overleaves gives one a window into self-knowledge and brings cosmic understanding and tolerance toward others. Below is an explanation of each of the overleaves from which our souls can choose to enable us to fulfill our agreements and evolve in each incarnation: the overleaf choice roles are goals, modes, attitudes, centers, and chief features.

These five major categories each have seven overleaf choices, with some being positive or negative.

GOALS

Acceptance or Rejection (Expression)
Growth or Retardation (Inspiration)

Dominance or Submission (Action)

Stagnation (Assimilation)

MODES

Power or Caution (Expression)

Passion or Repression (Inspiration)

Aggression or Perseverance (Action)

Observation (Assimilation)

ATTITUDES

Idealist or Skeptic (Expression)

Spiritualist or Stoic (Inspiration)

Realist or Cynic (Action)

Pragmatist (Assimilation)

CENTERS

Higher Intellectual or Intellectual (Expression)

Higher Emotional or Emotional (Inspiration)

Moving or Sexual (Action)

Instinctive (Assimilation)

CHIEF FEATURES

Greed or Self-Destruction (Expression)

Arrogance or Self-Deprecation (Inspiration)

Impatience or Martyrdom (Action)

Stubbornness (Assimilation)

In an early channeling session, Michael told me what my overleaves are in this present incarnation. My essence role is that of *scholar* (roles do not change from lifetime to lifetime, but the overleaves do), and I am a *mid-cycle mature* soul. I have a goal of *dominance* in the mode of *caution* and *deliberation*. My attitude is that of a *spiritualist* with emphasis on *verification*. This is probably why I am willing to struggle until I find acceptable answers to my basic questions. *Who am I? Why am I here?* I am operating from the *moving* center, which is being motivated by *emotion*. My chief feature is *stubbornness* with a secondary chief feature of *arrogance*. This might make sense to those of you who know me.

Developing an understanding of karma and its influence over our many lifetimes is very important. Michael says that we can choose each life experience from a place where we have an understanding of our previous lives, and we realize what lessons we need to experience next.

Some call this place heaven. Some call it paradise. From there, our soul chooses to enter a physical body shortly before or right after its birth. In other words, we choose our parents and the lessons to be learned in that lifetime.

Esoteric teachings tell us that reincarnation is one of the most important concepts to be grasped. The universe functions through reincarnation to advance the evolution of mankind. This evolution is not only physical but spiritual. I became comfortable with these ideas and completely lost any apprehension I had toward channeling voices from another dimension.

However, channelers must be careful to make sure that the entity they are in contact with is positive and helpful, as there are some dangerous and negative entities that could be contacted inadvertently. One could open a channel to a negative entity that deliberately gives false information in order to negate the validity of the answers given by positive entities.

While this knowledge is fascinating, after a while, it's just stuff unless we apply it to our present-moment consciousness. Knowledge is seductive. It's easy to begin thinking we know more than we really do about something that is probably way beyond our grasp in this dimension. However, this knowledge has made a great difference for me in this life. I try to see the essence of people, which helps me be less judgmental.

Meditation

As I searched spiritual concepts, theologies, and other dimensions, I began to find the answers I wanted. I came to realize that having religion or carrying a certain set of beliefs is not the same as being spiritual. Spirituality is the connection to God or a Higher Power. For me, that connection is possible with meditation. It is surrender to who I am in the moment as an intrinsic part of the universe. Eckhart Tolle tells us that when you surrender to what is and so become fully present, the past ceases to have any power. The realm of Being, which had been obscured by the mind, then opens up. Suddenly, a great stillness arises within you, an unfathomable sense of peace. And within that peace, there is great joy. And within that joy, there is love. And at the innermost core, there is the sacred, the immeasurable, That which cannot be named.[7]

A Moment without Thought

A moment without thought
And the background noise ceases
And I can suddenly hear
The silence between sounds
The silence beneath sound
From which all sounds emerge
Like waves from the sea.

A moment without thought
And the fog disperses
And the world is filled with translucent light
New dimensions of detail
And sharpness and colour and depth.

A moment without thought
And these suburban streets
Are a pristine new world
Like a garden glistening with dew
The morning after creation
As if a husk of familiarity

Has cracked and fallen away
Leaving naked primal isness.

A moment without thought
And I'm no longer standing separate
No longer an island but part of the sea
No longer a static centre
But part of the flowing stream.

A moment without thought
And the train has stopped between stations
And there was never any motion, never any track
A moment like a wormhole
Infinitely expanding
Like stepping through a narrow gate
To find an endless open plain
The panorama of the present.

And this new world of no-thought
Is neither alien nor unfamiliar
But a place where benevolence blows through the air
And soft shimmering energy fills every space
And the sunlight is the translucent white light of spirit
The deepest, closest, warmest place
The ground where I am rooted.

—by Steve Taylor[8]

VI.

WHY AM I HERE?

I Am Part of the Universal Oneness

The universe is a distinct, comprehensive, working system, always expanding, always changing. It contains everything that exists right now—all matter, energy, planets, galaxies, time, and space. Each of us inhabiting the planet is a manifestation of the universe as it exists in this moment. Eckhart Tolle in his book *A New Earth* tells us many times that to be conscious of this manifestation (connection to the universe), one must dwell in the present, not in the future or the past. *Our function in the universe is to realize that we are connected to everything in it. Our purpose here is to experience growth and to become conscious of being part of the universal oneness.*

Understanding this, I was able to make more sense of the philosophies of the major religions, including Christianity, and of the questions about who I am and why I am here. This concept of oneness, that we are all part of the same thing, is a concept that has been put forth by many people over the centuries.

I remember hearing about oneness as a youth in church. The Father, the Son, and the Holy Ghost are one example. The psalmist says in Psalm 133:1, "Behold, how good and how pleasant it is for brethren to dwell together in unity."[1]

Paul, with whom we began in Chapter 1, speaks to us again in Galatians, that "there is neither Jew nor Greek . . . slave nor free . . . male nor female; for you are all one in Christ Jesus . . . and heirs according to the [Creator's] promise" of unconditional love for humanity and all of creation.[2] If each of us realizes who we are and who the person standing next to us is—that *we are all one*—how can we help but love each other, help each other, and take responsibility for our planet?

Separation

(The Lord's Prayer Stanza 4)
And lead us not into separation, but
deliver us from forgetting that
within us is God's kingdom, power, and glory,
and that we are ONE WITH EVERYTHING!

So if it is true that we are all one and that universal oneness equals love, why are we not loving and connecting with each other?

Over the years, I have come to a better understanding of the pain of the planet and its inhabitants, reminiscent of the apple and the snake in the creation allegory. Adam and Eve lost their connection with the universe and, at the same time, with God and with each other. In other words, they became captivated by their egos. Our egos have been disconnecting us from oneness ever since.

I wonder, along with author/activist Rodney King after being brutally beaten by police, *Why can't we all just get along*? But we are still separate and, more recently with George Floyd's murder, still marching with banners reminding ourselves that "Black Lives [Do] Matter!" Why should we have to be reminded that another person's life matters, forgetting that we are all one and part of the same universe?

Religions and countries also have collective egos, which in some cases are very fragile. Certain that their belief systems and systems of government are the right ones, these collective egos separate groups of people from each other. I believe the religions of the planet with their many doctrines and dogmas not only cause deep separation between groups of souls but between individual souls and their connection with the Creator or oneness of the universe.

Sadly, religious wars are fought over differences in theology. The essence of the world's religions is oneness and love. If the nations' inhabitants really took the essence of religion to heart, there would be no war, and we would all live in peace. As it stands, our planet seems to be in a state of permanent unrest. For example, we suffer from a pandemic and overpopulation. We struggle with climate change and other environmental problems. We are experiencing renewed tension with China and our Muslim neighbors. We have recently experienced an attempted coup on our democracy, which makes clear the polarization between groups of people.

Where there is unity, or oneness, there is love, but the concept of oneness and love, so prevalent in all religions, is destroyed by the separation caused by the ego, as in us or them, Baptist or Mennonite, Catholic or Protestant, Democrat or Republican, Socialist or Communist, American or Chinese. We lose our oneness with God and each other when we so arrogantly hold up our belief system as the one truth. I am convinced there must be a better way of understanding our situation here on Earth. Teaching our children through stories and lengthy sermons embedded with dogma and masquerading as the truth is not helping the planet evolve.

I am as certain now as always that rigid belief systems separate us from each other, from our Creator, and from the universe, causing the endless pain and suffering on our planet, as referred to by poet Steve Taylor in the poem below, and I renew my vow to find the esoteric essence in all belief systems.

It's Hard to Be a Human Being

It's hard to be a human being
when you seem to be trapped inside yourself
with the rest of the world out there on the other side
and you feel insignificant and fragile, like a tiny island
surrounded by a vast roaring ocean
that's threatening to submerge you.

It's hard to be a human being
when you're forced to share your inner world
with a crazy whirling thought machine
that never stops churning and chattering
and makes you fear things that can't hurt you
and desire things that can't make you happy.

It's hard to be a human being
when you're so permeable to trauma
that ingrains itself deep inside you
and seems impossible to erase
and it's so easy to pick up attachments and habits
that grow stronger each time you express them
until they take over your life.

It's hard to be a human being
when the world is so chaotic and confusing
that you can't sense your right direction
or find a life that aligns with your purpose

so you feel inauthentic and unfulfilled
like an actor who hates the role she plays.

It's no wonder we feel restless and uneasy
as if this world isn't meant to be our home.
It's no wonder life seems a burden
and we spend so much time trying to escape from
ourselves.
It's no wonder we cause so much conflict
and leave trails of trauma everywhere we go.

But every strand of human hardship can be traced
back to the same source.

Our sufferings are the pains of separation.
We're lonely fragile fragments
who once felt part of the whole
and long for unity again.

Slow your life down
until you regain your sense of balance.
Let your mind fall silent
until you feel yourself reconnecting to the world.

And soon you will feel
the lightness of life living through you.

Soon you will sense
the harmony of belonging to the whole.

And then you will remember
how easy human life was meant to be.

—by Steve Taylor[3]

The Law of Love

One of the most interesting studies I found on my odyssey was a channeled entity named Ra from ancient Egypt. His philosophies date from before Bible times, yet they contain many of the teachings we presently find in major religions, including Christianity. Ra calls himself "a humble messenger of The Law of One."

The Ra material—a gift from another dimension—confirmed everything that I had been learning, bringing a depth of understanding beyond that of the entity Michael. Where Michael's answers tell of our existence here on Earth with regards to our present and past lives and soul journey, the Ra material answers questions about oneness on a cosmic level.

Ra tells us that there are two paths that we, of this density, choose on our journey evolving to higher dimensions. These are "service to self" and "service to others." When we have evolved to a high enough dimension, the souls in service to self and the souls in service to others will become one.

However, at present there is a constant rivalry between these two paths that tries to influence us in our dimension.

The answers given in channeling can come from either one of these groups. This is precisely why we must be sure that the channeled entity we are in contact with is from the service-to-others positive group and not from the negative service-to-self (also called Orion) group. Answers from the negative or service-to-self group are sometimes false and misleading and tend to negate or invalidate all channeling.

In other words, false answers given by the service-to-self group are designed to make one question the positive answers given by the service-to-others group.

Ra answers my questions about who I am and why I'm here. The simple concept of absolute oneness is what men and women on Earth must return to if they are to evolve. The idea of total unity with our brothers and sisters, regardless of who they are or how they might express themselves, is the original thought and purpose of the Creator.

Again, my concept of our purpose here is to evolve until we can move to the next dimension. We do that by looking back from that dimension after each lifetime and choosing a next life that will give us more understanding and bring us closer to God and being ONE WITH EVERYTHING, God included. Understanding the concept of heaven and hell was always a problem for me, but evolution and reincarnation are the concepts that encompass and modify the belief in heaven and hell.

I do believe that it is our duty to evolve in our understanding and connection to our Creator, Higher Power, God. For me, this involves being ONE WITH EVERYTHING, meaning understanding that we are all part of God and each other.

For the channeled entity Ra, love implies a unity so great that we see ourselves and everyone else as the Creator. Since we see each other as the Creator, we see one being, implying a unity not only with the Creator but with the universe and everything in it.[4]

I believe our planet would be a better place entirely if we could follow, without distortion, the simple essence of Ra's teachings, which is also the essence of the world's major religions, including Christianity. What is this essence? In three words, *we are one*!

How can we be connected to the universe and become part of the message of oneness?

When I began to be conscious of serving the planet and being more closely related to its evolution organically and spiritually, I learned from *The Law of One* that we evolve by not returning anger for anger, or sadness for sadness, but by offering compassion and comfort.[5]

This is why Jesus said to "resist not evil." I feel that not resisting evil means not using evil to counter evil forces. Not resisting evil is to become transparent to its force, letting it pass through us while understanding and working toward its alleviation. This brings to mind the wars we are fighting in this country, including the war on drugs and war on poverty. To resist or fight is to see someone as other than self, as other than the one Creator, and this is the negative path. The positive path sees and loves all as self and as one, which for me is the only path toward our evolution as a species in this dimension on this planet.

It is a gigantic universe, and if we have a true relationship to it, we must remember our oneness with it, even though as depicted in the following poem, we at times would prefer to relish our separateness. As we do remember our oneness with the universe and others, we will evolve and will assist those on the negative path to evolve with us.

The Wave

The ocean sighed with pleasure
as the wind caressed and stroked her and soon the
wave was born.

The wave felt his oneness with the ocean.

He felt her as his source, as part of his own being and
knew he could never exist apart from her.

But soon the wave began to watch himself. He
saw his own smooth and graceful motion and was
mesmerized.
He saw the beautiful bubbling foam that sprayed
around him and was transfixed.

The wave fell in love with himself.
He started to believe that he was his own master
that it was his own strength that was propelling him.
He believed that he was directing his own flow and
could change direction if he wanted.

The wave forgot the ocean, and saw himself as
separate—
a self-sufficient, sea-less wave.

He felt proud of his power, exhilarated by his
autonomy
as he rolled faster and rose higher.

But then he looked around and saw the other waves—
the ones who had already peaked and crashed
and were beginning to dip and to disperse and the
others who were already dissolving, disappearing.

The wave felt afraid, realizing that his form was
temporary
that his speed and power would ebb away
and soon he would dissolve and disappear as well.

He felt alone as he sensed the empty
Space around him
And saw the distance between him
And the other waves.
He felt threatened by the ocean's vastness
Now that he seemed to be separate from it.

The wave resisted and rebelled.
He tried to build up more momentum, to collect
more water
to roll more smoothly, to foam more spectacularly
to make himself so powerful that he would never
dissolve away

to make his form so perfect that he could escape
decay.

But soon he realized that he had no choice
that he had less control than he thought, less
strength than he thought.
He knew he couldn't resist the flow of life and hold
back time and tide.

The wave stopped grasping and pushing and felt the
relief of letting go
and the freedom of no longer trying.

After his majestic foaming rush
and the glorious crescendo of his breaking he gave
himself up to his ebbing fading flow and to the ease
of his descent.
And he was filled with the joy of acceptance.

The wave allowed his boundaries to soften and felt
his connection to every other wave and his oneness
with the whole of the ocean.

He felt the vast wholeness of the ocean within his
own being then as his own being.

And then the wave dipped, slowed down, and began
to dissipate.
Quietly and serenely, without fear or resistance he
gave himself to the tide
and became the ocean again
knowing that he had never been anything else.

—by Steve Taylor[6]

Meditation and the Law of Love

Ra tells us to grow our understanding through meditation. The further we travel the spiritual path, the more
meaningful we will find meditation. Meditation starts as
a simple process, as shown in the sitting meditation and
in the meditation on the Lord's Prayer, both found in
Chapter 3. Little by little, meditation can become a way of
understanding and connecting to the universe. Through
meditation, we can also reduce the illusion of separation
caused by our egos.

Ra advises us to meditate on the complete unity of ourselves, others, and our circumstances here on the planet.
Through self-analysis and meditation, we can find a way
to express love and oneness in our daily lives and to react
to the illusion of separation as the Creator would: with
the thought of love. "This was also done by the teacher
whom you know as Jesus. For insofar as you . . . feel at
one with those things which are difficult for you"—that is,

to surrender—"to that extent will those circumstances be alleviated. This . . . is due to the Law of Love."[7]

To reiterate Eckhart Tolle's words from Chapter 5:

> When you surrender to what is and so become fully present, the past ceases to have any power. The realm of Being, which had been obscured by the mind, then opens up. Suddenly, a great stillness arises within you, an unfathomable sense of peace. And within that peace, there is great joy. And within that joy, there is love. And at the innermost core, there is the sacred, the immeasurable, That which cannot be named.

VII.

—— AM I AN ALCOHOLIC? ——
AA AND CONNECTION
TO A HIGHER POWER

(The Lord's Prayer Stanza 3)
Give us this day our daily strength, and
forgive us our unconsciousness
as we forgive those who are ego-bound among us.

Welcome to Alcoholics Anonymous and the fellowship of change! By connecting to a Higher Power as we do in meditation, getting the voice of the ego out of the way, and asking for help, change is possible.

My plan had always been to retire after forty years of horn-playing and make room for someone else to enjoy that wonderful job. At the age of sixty-two, I would hopefully still be at the top of my playing. I could hardly wait to move back to Reedley and my farm on the Kings River where I would reconnect with relatives and friends from

83

my youth. I started thinking about designing a river house. I planned to start a new life away from performance and the big city.

After retiring, I began a long process of deactivating my solo horn persona. Horn-playing, after performing at that level for forty years, had become my identity, so when my career was over, I was left with a vacuum. I had to begin figuring out what my life would be about next. Performing was not who I was anymore. When people ask me if I still play, I just say, "Well, that's my past life. I'm in a different portion of life now."

But there was a problem. During my career, my drinking was limited to three nights a week because of my concert obligations. Retirement opened the possibility of alcohol seven nights a week, which would be the end of me. So, three years before I retired, I joined AA and gave up alcohol for the next twenty years.

The question in my mind was, Am I really an alcoholic? But I must say that the ideas and the fellowship of AA had a profound effect on my spiritual journey. I had witnessed tremendous healing in myself and others through AA and connecting to a Higher Power. There was magic in watching people separate themselves from old, addictive personalities and become connected to something outside themselves.

Almost every morning, I would ride my bike from my Mill Valley home down the bike path by the bay to a seven a.m. meeting at the cabin on Tennessee Valley Road. The concept of Higher Power at AA began to reconnect me to my early Christian training with a tolerance and understanding that I lacked in my youth. My objection to all religion, plus church and Sunday school, was that it could have been *simplified* to "know yourself and your relationship to the universe and a Higher Power" and to "love your neighbor as yourself."

By the way, I have my own Bible story I'd like to tell here. During the middle of my career, I was on tour in a strange city walking on the sidewalk, killing time in the afternoon before an evening concert. I looked down suddenly to find a Bible on the sidewalk. I immediately thought, *God is sending me a message here*. I reached down, picked up the Bible, and returned to my hotel room, planning to open it at random for a message from the Higher Power. I centered myself and carefully and randomly opened to find my message. What I got was many pages of so-and-so begat so-and-so, and so forth. My feeling at the time was one of relief that I could continue ignoring Christianity in general. See, I was right! Too many words.

While attending AA, my colleagues and friends in the symphony did notice a difference in my overall state of being. They told me I was more positive and upbeat. Giving up alcohol and being in fellowship with like-minded people was another life-changing experience of self-discovery.

Alcohol for me was a way of short-circuiting my judgmental ego that was addictive. Through the process of esoteric self-discovery, I have become much less reliant on this escape.

VIII

REEDLEY PEACE CENTER A NEW LIFE ON THE RIVER

War is insane, but it's something that we humans are addicted to. I am a pacifist, a remnant from my early Mennonite training. I, along with some friends from my youth, were interested in protesting our country's involvement in a new war. We formed the Reedley Peace Center.

The members of the Reedley Peace Center were people I had known from the church I grew up in and left almost fifty years earlier. We were of like mind protesting this new war. These same folks were members of a Sunday school class at the church, and I soon realized that we were looking for answers to the same questions. However, they were still deeply involved in finding answers in the Bible and Christianity. But they were busy making sense of Christianity in the church I had left. The church had changed, and I had changed. This Sunday school class and the church were at the same place philosophically that I had arrived at as far as being all-inclusive and tolerant of all races, faiths, and sexual orientations. The anti-war philosophy is what connected me to these people in a new and meaningful way.

So the Reedley Peace Center became my entrance back into the world of Christianity and the First Mennonite Church of Reedley, California. The peace center held weekly potluck meetings with wonderful, informative speakers for many years until the pandemic. We held anti-war protests and marches that greatly distressed the more conservative members of our church and community. During the pandemic, we have been holding Zoom meetings with about sixty people attending.

One evening, members of our peace center were holding a candlelight protest watch in the park in response to the Gulf War. It had been publicized. We were standing in a circle with our candles. Our pastor was with us. A Sequoia Safety Council ambulance drove by, its drivers protesting our protest by honking their horn and blowing their siren, yelling out the window at us to leave the country if we didn't like it.

While we were there, a large group of people from other churches, mostly Baptists, rushed at us in a threatening manner, calling us anti-American. There were about thirty of us, and I said to the group, "Let's kneel down with our candles." The group approached us, but they couldn't confront us because we were all kneeling. There's no way you can confront a group of people kneeling in a circle with candles lit.

Then the pastor from our church and their pastor talked and diffused the situation.

I always wondered how anyone who believes in Jesus's commandment to love your neighbor can not be horrified at the state of mankind on this planet.

Through being in contact with the wonderful souls at the peace center and the Sunday school class, I was able to find my way back into the church, a new kind of church where I was comfortable for the first time in my life discussing and debating the teachings of Jesus. In fact, I even joined the choir. However, after fifty years playing the horn (which is pitched in the key of F), to sing the right pitch, I had to transpose from the pitch I heard in my head.

At this stage in my life, I was beginning to understand the meaning of what Jesus said. It all made sense now in relation to what I had learned in my spiritual odyssey with teachers such as Tolle and Taylor, and from the other dimensions, Michael and Ra.

POSTLUDE

My Esoteric Spiritual Odyssey

Why are we here? To experience the drama and chaos of life in this dimension so we can learn lessons that will help us grow in understanding and prepare us for our next life.

Going from an ego-centered, separate, me-against-the-world state of mind to the place where we feel *oneness with everything* is the essence of enlightenment.

People think about Jesus in a very literal way. You need something of the other dimensions to be able to interpret and understand the meaning of his words; for example, when he says, "The meek will inherit the earth," I believe he is saying that those who rid themselves of ego will realize their oneness with everything. Finding the essence of a teaching is understanding its relationship to the oneness of everything.

Looking back, I see that I had to die and be resurrected, totally rejecting that body of beliefs from my youth and eventually coming to a place where I was comfortable in both my heart and my head and could love the essence of Jesus's teachings. I somehow have become comfortable with my current understanding of Jesus's teachings and any belief system that has love as its essence. This brings me back to what we were told in Sunday school—"God is love!"

As for the answers to my questions about who I am and why I'm here, I find no better answers than Eckhart Tolle's apt statement:

> You are not in the universe. You are the universe, an intrinsic part of it. Ultimately you are not a person, but a focal point where the universe is becoming conscious of itself. What an amazing miracle.

State of Being

The other day, I woke up *mad*! I was angry with everyone who has different beliefs and outlooks than I do, especially concerning vaccinations and the pandemic.

Somewhere in the back of my brain, there was an unconscious belief that anger would change things and make people come to my point of view. Having become a bit more conscious of that voice in my head that was creating this emotion, I realized that the anger was depleting me and serving no purpose whatsoever. The anger wasn't changing anything in the present except for my state of being.

What a gift, then, to realize that I did have a choice as to my state of being.

What I say is not what I do—most of the time. I'm hoping to do better, both in this life and in the next.

I was thinking today of that old joke, "What did the wise man say to the hotdog vendor?" He said something that I have realized this book is all about. Make me ONE WITH EVERYTHING!

Remembering Myself

Last night, sometime around three a.m., I was suddenly wide awake, my mind wandering through the past and dwelling on my ego-filled struggles. This regression into the past was probably prompted by the sight of an old colleague on Facebook. Once again, I was back in conflict and competition with this person and found myself planning some sort of negative event to challenge his ego and arrogance. What insanity this is! Why am I offended by someone I haven't seen or heard from in years? What does it have to do with me now? Why was this still keeping me awake at night? As I lay there, all the lies of my ego-fueled reality were suddenly in view. From the perspective of the work and *Practicing the Power of Now*, I saw how severely unconscious and meaningless these life struggles are. This glimpse was a gift, which is a crack in the dam of my ego reality. Maybe I can write a note of thanks to the person who unknowingly triggered this insight.

Meditation

Life has opened like a flower.
I have begun to see oneness.

Yet the ego-self is persistent.
I swim upstream toward oneness.
The current is strong,
yet with work I find areas of stillness.

Stillness is a gift that connects me to everything.
I seek that stillness when I remember to.

—by David Krehbiel

My Purpose

Why are we here?
To be with kindred souls,
to gather together for protection,
protection from the insanity of the world
around us.

Can we make a difference?
Does our small portion of life have any effect?
Can we remember the joy of experiencing this life?
Can we fall in love with the present moment?

—by David Krehbiel

THE END

NOTES

III. Creative Not Caring

1. Steve Taylor, "The Voice inside Your Head," in *The Calm Center: Reflections and Meditations for Spiritual Awakening* (Novato, CA: New World Library, 2015), 13.

2. David Christopher Lewis, "The Aura of the Great Central Sun: The Hub of Life," in *Advanced Studies of the Human Aura: How to Charge Your Energy Field with Light and Spiritual Radiance* (Livingston, MT: Meru Press, 2015), 16.

3. The Hearts Center, "Short Tube of Light," in *Pray, Sing, Dance and Play With Us* (Livingston, MT: The Hearts Center, 2011), 6.

4. Steve Taylor, "You Are Not the Process," in *The Clear Light: Spiritual Reflections and Meditations* (Novato, CA: New World Library, 2020), 78.

IV. Stepping Up the Search: Who Am I Now?

1. Don Elkins et al., *The Law of One: Book I: The Ra Material* (Atglen, PA: Whitford Press, 1984), 37.

2. Elkins et al., *The Law of One*, 38.

V. Connecting with the Universe: Guides along the Way

1. Deut. 10:14 (New King James Version).

2. 1 Kings 8:27 (New King James Version).

3. John 1:51 (New King James Version).

4. Eckhart Tolle, *Practicing the Power of Now: Essential Teachings, Meditations, and Exercises from the Power of Now* (Novato, CA: New World Library, 2001), 91.

5. Carlos Castaneda, *Journey to Ixtlan: The Lessons of Don Juan* (New York, NY: Washington Square Press, 1972), 135.

6. Chelsea Quinn Yarbro, *Messages from Michael: 25th Anniversary Edition* (Akron, OH: Cælum Press, 2005), 56.

7. Tolle, *Practicing the Power of Now*, 102.

8. Taylor, "A Moment without Thought," *The Calm Center*, 42–43, st. 1–2, 6.

VI. Why Am I Here?

1. Psalms 133:1 (New King James Version).

2. Galatians 3:28–29 (New King James Version).

3. Taylor, "It's Hard to Be a Human Being," *The Clear Light*, 33.

4. Elkins et al., *The Law of One*, 22.

5. Elkins et al., *The Law of One*, 244.

6. Taylor, "The Wave," *The Clear Light*, 108.

7. Elkins et al., *The Law of One*, 25.

——— ACKNOWLEDGMENTS ———

My sincerest thanks to Robert Enns (editing), Carol Krehbiel (administration), Paul and Ruth Buxman (editing and inspiration), Matt Krause (editing), Marilyn Bone Kloss (book design/editing), and most of all, R. A. Krause for co-writing and editing.

ABOUT THE AUTHOR

David Krehbiel began his musical career playing the trumpet in elementary school, using his musical talents to cover up his scholastic shortcomings. He soon, however, discovered the French horn, loved the sound, and never looked back. As a freshman at Fresno State in California, he became a member of the newly formed Fresno Philharmonic. At the beginning of his senior year in 1957, carrying his horn and a suitcase holding all his belongings, he boarded the train to Evanston, Illinois, where he had transferred, to attend Northwestern University and study with the renowned French horn teacher Philip Farkas. In 1958, he auditioned for Dr. Fritz Reiner, conductor of the Chicago Symphony Orchestra, who hired him as an extra. After a short time, Krehbiel, the youngest member of the Chicago Symphony Orchestra, was appointed assistant principal French horn for Farkas, his teacher.

In 1963, he was invited to be principal horn of the Detroit Symphony, where he played and taught at Wayne State University for nine years. For the next twenty-six years, he was the principal horn of the San Francisco Symphony, where he taught at the San Francisco Conservatory of Music and the Music Academy of the West. After retiring as principal horn, he taught for a time at the Colburn School in Los Angeles, where he was awarded an Honorary Doctorate. He was a founding member and later conductor of Summit Brass and has been a conductor and soloist at many International Horn Workshops.

He lives with his wife, Carol, in their hometown of Reedley, California, on their farm overlooking the Kings River.

R.A. Krause,
Co-Writer and Editor

Ruth Anne Krause, owner of RA Krause Writing and Editing, lives in Reedley, California, where she writes, edits books, and coaches writing. She is a former instructor of English composition and literature and lives with her husband, Jim, and their cat, Eleanor.

HEARTS to be **HEARD**

Giving a Voice to Creativity!

With every donation, a voice will be given to the creativity that lies within the hearts of our children living with diverse challenges.

By making this difference, children that may not have been given the opportunity to have their Heart Heard will have the freedom to create beautiful works of art and musical creations.

Donate by visiting

HeartstobeHeard.com

We thank you.

Remove this page and cut out the bookmarks below.
Line up the pieces back-to-back and glue or laminate them together.
May these words of wisdom give you daily strength.

Side A | Side B

Side A

The moment that **JUDGEMENT** stops through acceptance of what is, you are **FREE OF THE MIND.**

WHAT IS GOD?

THE ETERNAL ONE LIFE UNDERNEATH ALL THE FORMS OF LIFE.

WHAT IS LOVE?

TO FEEL THE PRESENCE OF THAT ONE LIFE DEEP WITHIN ALL CREATES.
TO BE IT.
THEREFORE, ALL LOVE IS THE LOVE OF GOD.

Side B

The moment contains **LOVE.**
The universie is **ONE BEING.**
Gaze into the mirror,
See the **CREATOR.**
Gaze at the Creation,
See the **CREATOR.**

ACCEPTANCE –
                    NON RESISTANCE
ENJOYMENT –
                    NON JUDGEMENT
ENTHUSIASM –
                    NON ATTACHMENT

"You are not **IN** the universe; you **ARE** the universe—an intrinsic part of it. Ultimately you are not a person, but a focal point where the universe is becoming conscious of itself. What amazing miracle."

—Echart Tolle

Made in the USA
Middletown, DE
26 November 2022

15713653R00071